The Bootneck BluePrint

By Craig Williams
AKA The Renegade Bootneck

Contents

Thank You

Dear Future Bootneck,

First of all thanks for purchasing The Bootneck Blueprint. It is likely that you have been using my website, blog, FB page and Twitter feed as a valuable resource during your journey to what I believe is the greatest career in the British Military. If that is the case, you understand I aim to give you the very best RM related information to ensure the Corps continues to get the cream of today's youth.

I am very proud of my 15 years service with the Royal Marines, which was dramatically cut short in 2008. Royal Marines are a unique breed and it takes a very special person to become one.

I promise to continually strive to provide valuable information and advice so I won't waste my time talking about how great the Marines are… I must however mention that the selection process is extremely tough. There is a very good reason why the Corp has used the strap line "99.9% need not apply" in a recent recruitment campaign.

I hope you find this guide valuable and welcome any kind of feedback you may have. Before we go any further I want to pass on two tips that have served me incredibly well in life.

Remember:

1 - Everyone has something to teach you!
2 - You should try to test yourself in some way… everyday!

Yours in pursuit of excellence,

Craig Williams
The Renegade Bootneck.

Bootneck Blueprint

The 'No BS' guide to maximising your chance of winning your Green Beret!

If you're thumbing through this book you're already showing that you have many of the facets required to stand proud amongst some of the fittest, most professional and hardest fighting soldiers in the world.

These characteristics include;

- Industrious
- Relentless in pursuit of your goals
- Committed
- Dedicated
- Audacious

Good work, but sadly they're not going to be enough. Royal Marines basic training is reputed to be the longest and most arduous basic training in the western world, but at this stage you probably already know that?!

What you will not, and cannot, know is whether you are one of the .01% of men that will triumph!

Captured in these pages are the most comprehensive Royal Marines joining secrets ever compiled. I have spent countless hours, days, weeks and months interviewing those that know! Subject matter experts that steer training, mould recruits and create physical machines primed for combat. Until now the information contained in this dossier was a closely guarded secret. What's more, I have coupled my own knowledge and experience amassed through over a decade of service allowing you to stack the odds in your favour.

The information chronicled below will not only maximise your chances of successfully completing the toughest 32 weeks imaginable, but seriously give you the ability to 'walk it'! With insider secrets so powerful, it would not surprise me if Britain's elite actually changed training to combat its effectiveness.

Previously writing as 'The Renegade Bootneck' to protect my identity, I will give you a step by step, no bullshit guide to preparing your mind and body for Royal Marines basic training.

'I wish I could tell you that I was a super recruit...'

I wish I could tell you that I was a super recruit with a chiselled physique that excelled at every aspect of the 32 week program. That fitness was a breeze, marching was a walk... er... on the parade ground and I took to soldiering like a duck to water, but I didn't. I was very much the average Joe.
Probably a lot like you?

In honesty, I struggled through every step of the way. My mind was in such a whirl when I joined that I don't even remember arriving at the Commando Training Centre in Lympstone! I was so out of my depth I would lay awake at night wondering where the hell I was. Everything from the instructors to the atmosphere filled me with dread. The culture shock was overwhelming, but I held in and went on to have the greatest years of my life, with the greatest friends and colleagues in the world.

'If only I had had help before I got there'

If only I had had help before I got there. I now know that with just a few pieces of key advice I could have made things so much easier for myself. In fact I could have significantly increased my chances of success and may have even won the coveted Kings badge.

Luckily I, like 95% of recruits scraped through. I was fortunate that I had the ability to learn quickly and had slightly above average fitness. I then went on to have a fantastic career, have friends that are closer than family and can now hold my head high proud that I passed for duty in Britain's Elite – I earned my Green Beret!!!

DISCLAIMER:

Reading this alone is NOT enough to get you through. I will simply give you tools to maximise your chance of getting through... you will have to put each of these renegade secrets in to practice. At this point I want you to know just how hard you are going to have to work, you have to develop a desire to win a Green Beret that is so powerful that nothing will stand in your way... not homesickness, fatigue, hunger, thirst, injury and definitely not the Commando tests.

Introduction

This book is split into a number of sections aimed at preparing both mind and body to join the Royal Marines. I have consulted my closest network of friends and professional colleagues to bring you these secrets from those at the very heart of recruit training. I have scoured the online forums to find out what people want and need to know, but also to find the biggest myths surrounding the route to one of the world's most elite forces. I make no apologies for the next paragraph as it really must be said.

First step and message to today's youth

Namby pamby mummy's boys, spoilt and arrogant brats – Forget it! There is no room in the Royal Marines for the spoilt teens that parade around in the most expensive gear and have their parents and grandparents do everything for them. Regardless of how much of a man you THINK you are, you're arrogant, know it all, expect it all and not prepared to work for 'fuck all' attitudes will not serve you well in the Royal Marines. The world does not owe you and your not just gonna get given your beret you have to earn it.

The Royal Marines have spent a considerable amount of time working ways to weed out those that are weak. I have personally thrashed many for being 'Jack', lazy, gobby and arrogant, that cannot feed themselves, look after themselves, think COD is war and war is COD. Now is the time to be honest with yourself…

Do you get yourself up in the morning for work or for school? Do you iron? Can you do the laundry? Do you do the washing up regularly? Do you keep your room tidy? And do you do all those things without being nagged for hours before you get up off your jumped up arse and put in a super lame effort in the hope you never get asked again?

If you answered yes to most of these question you maybe one of the 'cream' of today's youth that the Royal Marines are looking for. If not, I believe you will do one or two things. You will giggle to yourself, proud in the fact that you are a lazy little shit or, hopefully you will think, no I don't do those things, but you know what… I will from now on! And you have just taken the first step to joining the ultimate fighting soldier.

Part One

Know the Enemy

Section 1: The Royal Marine Commando selection process

The selection process for becoming a Royal Marines Commando consists of the following elements:

Step 1
Contact the Careers Advisors

Step 2
Armed Forces Careers Office visit

Step 3
Aptitude test

Step 4
Interview and medical check

Step 5
Pre-joining fitness test

Step 6
Potential Royal Marines Course (PRMC)

Step 1 – Contact the Careers Advisors

Ok, it's time for action. Do not be one of the thousands that get to their forties and regret never taking the first step to joining the Royal Marines. Get over to your local Royal Navy careers office. Remember that first impressions count, so dress accordingly and speak to the recruitment advisor in a polite and courteous manner. There is nothing wrong with you addressing them as Sir or Ma'am, and if you do, you will be creating a positive impression right from the start. An ability to display how respect for regimentation and for people in positions of authority is the first step in getting through the door and also a great way to stand out among today's youth.

When speaking to the recruitment advisor, he or she may ask you a number of initial questions relating to whether or not you have any criminal convictions, or whether you have or have had asthma at any time during your life. It is important that you are honest at every stage of the process. If you are not, they could find out at a later point and this may jeopardise your chances.

A couple of basics… also known as 'common dog fuck' in the Marines!!!

- Have a pen and paper to take notes during your initial telephone call.
- Have an up to date calendar or diary at hand to check suggested assessment and interview dates.
- Note of any meeting dates and ask questions if you are unsure about parking or directions etc.
- Read the information packs you are sent thoroughly. It will contain lots of important information about life within the Royal Marines including a choice of careers. During the interview you will be asked questions relating to the information contained within the recruitment literature.

Step 2 – Armed Forces Careers Office visit

Your initial meeting with the Royal Marines Careers Advisor is as important as any other and it is an opportunity for you to create a positive impression. Don't be late; remember arriving on time in the Marines is 'late'. Always aim to get their five minutes before your appointment. If you are going to be late, don't worry, just let the careers office know… oh… and have a good reason for it!!!

"I think, Not to ask questions even though you thought they were reasonable…" Corporal why are we using Large Packs when in 2 weeks we go to a unit and have to adapt to using a proper Bergen" (thrashed for that one!)"

J, Serving Bootneck (at time of print) DL

'Common dog' for your appointment

- Check the route to the Careers Office prior to any scheduled meeting.
- If you are travelling by car make sure you know where to park, or if you are taking public transport then check train/bus times as these can be unreliable.
- Note the Careers Office telephone number or better still enter it into your phone, just in case.
- Turn your phone off or at least put it on silent.

Step 3 – Aptitude test

The aptitude test is designed to assess your ability to work effectively with:

- Language
- Numbers
- Reasoning
- Mechanical comprehension

Check out the sample test questions at http://bootneckblueprint.com/rnrt/ and use the mock questions posted on the RM Facebook page to help you prepare.

Step 4 – Interview and medical check

Prepare to be interviewed both at the Armed Forces Careers Office (AFCO) and later on in the selection process. I remember practicing a few times which definitely helped. Once you have passed the interview you will need to undertake a medical check to make sure that you are in good health.

They will want to know all about you, especially:

- Why you want to become a Royal Marines Commando?
- What you have done to research it?
- How do you think you will cope with the training?
- Do you have any criminal offences?

Step 5 – Pre-joining fitness test (PJFT)

Many candidates fail the Potential Royal Marines Course (PRMC) during the 3-mile run. Therefore, the Royal Marines want to be sure that you can pass this prior to sending you down to Lympstone.

The PJFT consists of two runs on a running machine at a 2° incline. Specifically:
- 2.4km to be completed within 12mins 30secs
- 2.4km be best effort, but within *10mins 30secs, with a minute rest in between the two runs.

Northern Ireland PJFT ;
Run on terrain in 12mins 30sec then second in sub 10min (not on a treadmill!!)
Then 50 press-ups, 80 sit-ups and 4 pull-ups

*I recently interviewed the Sergeant Major of the PRMC, check out the post at royalmarinestraining.com. He stated that though the criteria is 10mins 30secs, a recruit

MUST complete the run in around 9mins and 30secs to get a good solid score and realistically be fit enough to get through.

Completing your PJFT

I suggest you do the first run at a speed of 12km per hour in order to complete it in just under 12.5 mins and reserve energy for the 2nd part. Ramp the speed up to at least 15km per hour for the second part, but remember it's a best effort so treat it as such.

Training for the PJFT

The first stage of the run is usually quite easy. It takes me around 1.5 miles to get into my stride for any run, but if there is any doubt of your ability to pass it… Remember… Practice, practice, practice!

REMEMBER: the second part of the run is considered a 'best effort' effort run. The assessor will expect you to work as hard as you can so DO NOT try to pace yourself or cruise to the finish line. Give it your all, aim for under 9.5 mins for the best possible score.

Follow these steps to get your run right…

Step 1 – Find your course. I recommend training for the run each day. Accurately measure 1.5 miles from your home or complete the test on a track. Though the test will be done on a treadmill, you only need to practice it on a treadmill a couple of times to get used to how running on a machine feels and to learn how to pace yourself initially.

Step 2 – Ease into it. Don't expect to burst out of the blocks like Usain Bolt straight away. It will take a few weeks for your heart and lungs to get accustomed to the stress and though your speed will increase relatively quickly, your leg muscles require a certain amount of time to build strength and endurance.

Step 3 – Mix it up – don't fall foul as many do to just doing the same route, same speed in the same kit week in, week out. I suggest interval training to help build cardiovascular fitness and leg strength quicker and avoid capping your efforts at 1.5 miles.

Suggested sessions – Download the Gymboss timer app to help you. The Tabata intervals will already be programmed in; other timings will need to be entered afterwards.

Tabata sprints

Complete the 1.5 mile run in 15 mins as a warm up. Then do no less than 8 rounds of 20 seconds as fast as possible followed by 10 seconds steady pace. Run the remainder of the 1.5 mile at a steady pace as a cool down.

Hill repeats

Find a steep hill approx 4-500m in length. Sprint up and jog down. Repeat for no less than 3 times. Challenge yourself to complete more than 5 hill sprints.
Shorter hills can be used, but more reps must be completed.

Running for time

Complete the 1.5 mile run in 15 mins as a warm up. Then, instead of stopping after 1.5 miles try to run as far as you can in 10.5 mins. Measure your distance with a pedometer app or on MapMyRun.com. Rest for a day and try to beat your distance.

Hare & hounds

Option 1 – BEGINNER – Complete the 1.5 mile run in 15 mins as a warm up with your training buddy.

At the turn around point get your buddy to return at the same pace, but give him a 3 minute head start. Try to catch up with your buddy before he crosses the line. This can also be done on two running machines side by side. As your time improves, increase the head start.

Option 2 – INTERMEDIATE – ask your buddy to run a 1.5 mile route in 15 mins. Give him a 3 minute head start and try to catch up with him before the turnaround point.
At the turnaround point either change roles or repeat.

Hurricane runs

The following intervals are similar to the winds in a storm, hence the name 'Hurricane'. The workout starts relatively easy and rapidly builds to an extended rest period in the middle… The 'eye of the storm'… Before the intensity falls to the start. The whole session takes around 8 minutes. Complete just one round if you are a beginner. Add additional rounds as you improve.

Time in seconds:

Sprint	steady jog
15	45
30	30
45	15
60	60
60	15
45	30
30	45
15	–

Fartleks

Run no less than 3 miles in total. Run the first ten minutes at a steady pace as a warm up then walk to the first lamp post, jog to the second and run to the third. As you advance jog to the first, run to the second and sprint to the third.
Alternatively jog for three, run for two and sprint for one.

Step 6 – The Potential Royal Marines Course (PRMC)

The Potential Royal Marines Course lasts for 3 days, during which time you will be assessed many times. You will also meet some recruits from the 'Kings Squad', the senior troop in training at the time. They will give you a better understanding of what training is really like. At the end of day three, the training team will let you know whether they think you have what it takes to begin Royal Marines Commando training. If you pass, you will receive a joining date. As it is the first major hurdle I have described the PRMC in more depth below.

WTF is the PRMC?

The Potential Royal Marines Course (PRMC) is a test of your suitability to become a Royal Marines Commando. As you can imagine, it is very hard to pass and is designed to MAKE YOU OPT OUT!!!

Don't let that put you off. It is only 3 days and though you will ache like nothing else afterwards completing it successfully is something to be proud of and the first real accomplishment in your quest to be a Royal Marine.

The instructors are looking for good all-rounders that DO NOT give up, show them that you have the potential to be one of the most feared, professional and respected soldiers in the world.

Remember – Pain is temporary, but quitting lasts forever!

Mentally there is only so much you can do to prepare. Even with the tips and advice I have listed in this guide, a great deal will boil down to just how much you want to be a Bootneck. Physical preparation is the easy part. Any young man with the aptitude and desire to pass out of training can and anyone can get themselves fit enough to pass the PRMC and eventually earn a green lid.

Concentrate on the following in preparation for your PRMC:

- Press-ups
- Sit-ups

- Pull-ups
- Multi-stage fitness test
- Medium to Long distance endurance runs
- Swimming

Implement these into your daily routine and you'll have a far greater chance of succeeding at the PRMC. Always adhere to the best possible form and technique.

What does the PRMC consist of?

The Potential Royal Marines Course (PRMC) takes place at the Commando Training Centre Royal Marines (CTCRM), Lympstone in Devon. It is used to assess, as it says, your 'potential' to be a Royal Marine. CTCRM is located near to Exmouth and by the time you make your way through the gates you will buzz from the atmosphere. This is the place where Commandos are forged and now it is your turn.

This is your chance. DO NOT go unprepared and half arsed, but also remember that this is a great opportunity for you to have a look at the Royal Marines to see if it suits you as much as it allows the instructors to check out your abilities.

The PRMC timetable

To begin with let's take a look at what you will go through during the PRMC.

You will get all the basic information about the PRMC in your course joining instructions including what to take and how to prepare. Make sure you read it carefully and then follow the instructions as directed.

The PRMC is designed to make you opt out and give in. It will be harder than anything you have ever done.

The average course has 60 potential recruits all bidding for a spot. Current averages are 35 lads per course make it through and 10 of these progresses through training and eventually gain their green beret. The odds are kinda stacked against you, but reading this guide and implementing the steps is a great way of changing that and remember… if you make the grade you will pass, you're not in direct competition with anyone other than yourself.

Arrival

When you arrive at the PRMC you will be met straight away by the Duty Instructor. As soon as you get off the train he will be waiting for you. He will take a roll call before briefing you on your next movements. Remember to listen to everything he tells you. You are being assessed right from the word go and you must be able to follow his instructions to the letter. For God's sake don't fidget!

Though the instructors understand that you are a civilian they will expect a smart appearance, some discipline and maturity. Turn up wearing smart formal clothes such as a shirt, tie and trousers. Not jeans, t-shirts and Trainers! Polish your shoes and don't put your hands in your pockets, stand up straight and do not fidget. It may feel awkward at first, but not as awkward as doing press ups as punishment.

Oh and don't turn up chewing gum!!!

Following registration you will be issued clothing and boots to wear during the PRMC and also receive a briefing on what you will go through during the course.

Meal times

The main galley at CTCRM can be a bit of a foreboding place. Hairy arsed chefs love nothing more than jumping down the throat of new recruits and members of the PRMC. During the remainder of this guide I will explain why it is important to eat a good nutritional meal, but during the PRMC remember one thing… Eat like a bastard!!! Get as much down you as you can physically stomach without making yourself nauseous during the physical tests.

I also recommend that you drink plenty of water in order to prevent dehydration, and to help maintain concentration levels and performance.

The PRMC timetable – Day 1

Time to get busy! The day will begin at 6am, when you will have to get up, get showered, shaved, dressed and clean the room before going for breakfast and moving to the gym for the first test.

1.5 mile run, best effort

The first test consists of two runs;
- 1.5mile (2.4km) to be completed within 12mins 30secs as a squad.
- 1.5mile (2.4km) best effort, but within *10mins 30secs, with a minute rest in between the two runs.

Anyone who takes longer than 10 minutes 30 seconds will fail the course.

*Scoring system

10.31 or longer = Fail
10:11 to 10:30 = 1
09:51 to 10:10 = 2
09:31 to 09:50 = 3
09:11 to 09:30 = 4
08:51 to 09:10 = 5
08:50 or less = 6

Top tips

- Smaller lads get to the front to help with your smaller stride pattern.
- Use your arms during the walking portion to the help maintain momentum and listen to the PTI who will call out the step.
- Running in step with other people seems easy, but can be quite tough. Practise before you get there.
- Keep up and do not allow gaps to form. Gaps cause a 'caterpillar' type effect and will make it harder for not only you, but also the rest of the squad.
- Do not hold back on the run. Go all out to complete it in your fastest time possible.

As mentioned previously, the Sergeant Major in charge of the PRMC recently stated that a minimum time of 9mins 30secs is required to get a good solid score. Previously the score from your PJFT went towards your finally gym test results. However this changed in the latter part of 2013 as good runners would max the run then cruise in the gym.

Multi-stage fitness test.

You are required to reach level 13 during this part of the test, which is usually carried out during the afternoon of the first full day.

Multi-stage fitness test *scoring system

9.4 or less = fail
9.5 = 1
9.6 to 9.9 = 2
10 to 10.11= 3
11 to 11.8 = 4
11.9 to 12.5 = 5
12.6 or more = 6

Press-ups.

You will be required to perform as many press-ups as you can within 2 mins. Remember that the correct technique for the Royal Marines will be very different than what you would expect. Many recruits lose points during the press ups for not doing the correct technique and allowing the hips or shoulders to rise separately. The body MUST remain fixed throughout.

Press up test *scoring system

18 or less = fail
19 = 1
20 to 25 = 2
26 to 32 = 3
33 to 44 = 4
45 to 52 = 5
53 or more = 6

The correct press up technique

1 - Adopt the press up position with the weight on your hands and toes.
2 - Legs and arms outstretched with the hands directly under the shoulders.
3 - Keeping the body straight at all times.
4 - Lower your chest down to meet another candidate's fist.
5 - Press with the hands and return to the start position.
6 - Completely straighten and lock out your arms.
7 - Elbows remain close into your sides throughout.

Sit-ups.

You will be required to perform as many sits-ups within 2 minutes as you can, again using the correct technique.

Many recruits lose points during the sit ups as they fail to employ the correct technique and allow the knees to separate, allow their fingers to come away from the temples and fail to touch the knees with the elbows.

Sit up test *scoring system

24 or less = fail
25 = 1
26 to 32 = 2
33 to 40 = 3
41 to 50 = 4
51 to 65 = 5
66 or more = 6

The correct sit up technique

1 - Lie back on the floor, legs bent to 5 degrees (another candidate will hold your feet).
2 - Your fingers must stay in contact with the sides of your head.
3 - Your elbows must make contact with the mat on the downward motion.
4 - On the upward motion your elbows must come up to touch the knees.
5 - Keep the knees tight together throughout the exercise.

Pull-ups.

You will be required to perform up to 8 pull-ups using an overhand grip.

Pull up test *scoring system

0 – 3 = Fail
4 = 2
5 = 3
6 = 4
7 = 5
8 or more = 6

The correct pull up technique

Your body will hang straight whilst holding on to a wooden beam. You must pull yourself up until your chin is over the beam. This exercise is carried out to audible beeps, which is used to ensure discipline during the exercise and also prevent you from using swinging motions to pull yourself up. You must keep in time with the beeps.

Assault course

At first glance the assault course seems to be a test of your physical ability on a selection of obstacles. In truth, potential recruits are not insured for the complete obstacle course and ropes so the bottom field assault course is now a test of your determination and personal qualities. The ONLY criteria portion of the assault course is scaling the high obstacle course. Many recruits fail to negotiate the high planks because of a lack of confidence at height. It is impossible to describe exactly what the session will entail as the PTI's have the ability to throw in whatever they want. Once the high obstacle course is complete… the PTI's get to play.

The session will begin with the mother of all warm up's and a great deal of stamina will be required to complete the session. Baby carries, piggy backs, crawling, scaling walls and generally running will definitely feature along with press ups, sit ups, squats and a range of other exercises aimed at getting you wet, muddy and extremely tired.

Do not give up!

Bottom Field work out – Pass/Fail (Simples!)
High obstacle course – Pass/Fail (Simples!)

Endurance course

The endurance course is extremely tough and accounts for a very high percentage of people either failing or opting out.

You will complete the course in large groups and negotiate the tunnels, infamous sheep dip and Peters Pool in groups of about ten. PTI's will keep the others 'busy' as your group negotiate the obstacle.

Halfway through the Endurance course you will hit a large fire break in the moorland. This area will be used to really start to weed out the weaker members of the course. Strong members will receive very little attention, but if you are on a sticky wicket and look like you may give up they will keep applying the pressure until you give in.

The key to passing this element is keeping up with the lead group or 'pack', however tired you feel. You will be watched closely and assessed to see if you can operate effectively whilst pushing yourself to the limit.

Expect everything to be screaming for you to stop. At this point your internal dialogue, which I speak about later in this book, will be literally begging you to give in, don't let it get the better of you.

Endurance course *scoring system

Fail to complete = 0
V. Weak = 1
Weak = 2
Average= 3
Above Ave = 4
Good = 5
V. Good = 6

Swimming assessment

The swimming assessment is NOT a criteria test, though your final score will be affected if you are a weak swimmer. The test seems harder than it is, so don't psych yourself out of it. The aim is to jump into a swimming pool from a 5 meter board and swim a length of the pool using breaststroke, before treading water for 2 minutes.

Swimming can be improved with a small amount of training, so get a couple of sessions under your belt before you get down to Lympstone.

Swimming assessment *scoring system

25 metres = 1
50 metres = 2
75 metres = 3
100+ metres = 4

*The complete scoring system is correct as of Jan 2014

Passing PRMC

The current total scoring system for the PRMC is:

Fail = 21 or less
B = 22-29
A =30+

Swim score cannot be used to reach the minimum 22 pass/fail criteria

Pass rate

The current pass rate for the PRMC is 35 out of 60, just over 50%. The majority of people opt out for various reasons. Some find that the military just isn't right for them or realise that they miss home, are not quite as fit as they thought and some feel they are just not ready for it. There will be times when you feel like giving up, but the important thing is to think about the reasons you want to join the most Elite fighting force in the world and if you want it… keep going regardless. Remember that this is just the recruitment phase and IS NOT a true indication of life in the Royal Marines after training.

If you reach the end of the course then there is a strong possibility that you will be offered a Recruit Troop joining date. At the time of writing this, the waiting time or 'header time' as it is known, is about 3 months.

If you are unsuccessful (believe it or not, they are not allowed to say you have failed as it isn't PC) on your PRMC then you will be offered the opportunity to try again in the future. Your strengths and weaknesses will be explained and you will be told what you need to work on to be successful next time.

"You can be as fit as you like or as knowledgeable as you like but without fortitude, determination and an ability to get on with it and with each other you will never complete the 32 weeks as a lone wolf. The Corps still attracts the same calibre men as it did then and as it did with our fore bearers and the Corps values and ethos are something that will always be the building block to becoming not just a Royal Marine but a 'Bootneck'"

M, Serving Bootneck (at time of print)

Part Two

Preparing the Mind

Part Two

Section 2.1: Obtaining a Commandos Mind

Where most potential Royal Marines recruits go wrong is they spend a lot of time preparing their body, not always in the most efficient way either, and spend very little time preparing their minds. Mental toughness is going to be the primary weapon in getting you through basic training. Without mental toughness you are doomed to failure. It is not something you are born with and if you haven't got it don't fret. It can be developed and developed quickly.

In this respect I was lucky. I had not been sheltered from hard work and other stresses as I was growing up. I spent a lot of my childhood working the fields and farms high on the Pennine hills. I was no stranger to cold wet conditions, hard graft and loneliness. Cheerfulness under adversity is just one of the components of the Commando ethos and is required because bad weather, homesickness and even downright institutionalised bullying (plus more) will plague you throughout training.

Renegade top tip –Test yourself!

Every day you can test yourself in one way or another. You never know your limits until you push the boundaries and get out of your comfort zone. Obviously be sensible about it and although sometimes a little risk of harm is inevitable, but test yourself in ways that are controllable. Often I would end a heavy training session or even start the day with an ice cold shower. But that's stupid right? Maybe not. If you know how it feels to get up at 0500 force your tired limbs under a Baltic shower that steals your breath with the option of whacking up the temperature when it gets too much… it will be a doddle when you have to do it for real in the Corps.

Looking back at my time in training, I now recognise that much of the stress is self-imposed. Many serving Commandos will agree that we all spent a considerable amount of time worrying about what actually might not happen.

Dit Creep – Remember the party game 'Chinese whispers'? Well it happens in Royal Marines training too. A rumour starts and grows each time it is passed along. This can have a seriously damaging and de-motivating effect on nods (NOD – Sang name for a Royal Marines recruit. Originates from the Noddy style hat worn during the commando phase of training and the fact that they are constantly falling asleep during lessons).

Consider a recruit hears a trainer flippantly mention they should get the lads out of their beds tonight. Even at the first Chinese whisper, the message can be changed; the first recruit tells another that he overheard the trainer state they were GOING to get the lads out of bed. If the second recruit adds a small embellishment, 'dit creep' begins. Eventually, the entire troop stay awake and miss out on sleep in anticipation of the event they are so sure is going to occur. Always remember 'dit creep' and remember that nothing is ever as bad as it seems.

Renegade top tip - You will never second guess what is coming next so stop trying to.

The training team will go out the way to dislocate you from your expectations. The best way to combat this is to concentrate on the things that are definitely going to happen. When you have the opportunity to get inside your sleeping bag… get in it. I lost lots of valuable rest sitting and shivering on my Bergen waiting for the next thunder flash to go off and the order to 'Crash Move' to ring through the harbour area. After spending time on a training team I now know that the troop commander and troop sergeant offer a considerable amount of support to the recruits and if they feel they have had a tough day and need the rest will prevent the corporals from interfering with their rest.

Top ten ways to test yourself

During Royal Marines basic training you will be exposed to the following list many times, sometimes every day. The training team will devise ways to increase the stress that each of these things bring about.

1 – Sleep deprivation

Sleep deprivation has many effects on the body from disorientation to eventual death. Sleep deprivation is inevitable during training as well as in the mainstream Corps. It may be no surprise that one explanation for a recruit's nickname of 'Nod' has its origins in a constant nodding action due to lack of sleep. Sleep deprivation prevents you from thinking clearly and can, in severe cases, cause hallucinations. Find out how far you can go without sleep. Learn to recognise the effect it has on you so you can recognise the signs and symptoms. Finally… recruits falling asleep during lectures are dealt with quite heavily. The training team will always tell the troop to stand up if you are feeling sleepy. My advice is 'do it'. The minute you feel drowsy, stand up. If the instructor hasn't expressed his permission to stand up, politely ask for permission. No one will turn you down and you will probably get credit for being proactive.

2 – Tight deadlines

Recruit training is laced with periods when you have tight deadlines from rapid fire uniform changes known as 'Quick Changes' to inspections that is completely unachievable. The key is not to concentrate on achieving everything. You will be far more productive by concentrating on the things that really matter. Work out what is best, a few press ups for being two minutes late or being thrashed senseless and charged for a rusty weapon?

It is also essential that you get more done than the person next to you, but also essential that you help those that are struggling whenever you can.

3 – Heavy workload

Get used to some hard work. If like me you have grown up with regular work that would have been known as slavery 100 years ago, then no doubt you will be ok. If not, get out and find some hard graft. Labouring for a local builder, helping a farmer or even doing jobs around the house, tasks quicker than the average person would help you nurture an ability to work hard for long periods. Never shy away from hard work during training.

4 – Physical fatigue

During your preparation, try to push your limits to a point of physical fatigue. Learn to recognise the effects of fatigue which will help you combat the symptoms. If you know why you are a little confused you can do something about it.

5 – Mental fatigue

Ok, think about school. Think about all the revision you had to do before your exams. Now times those feeling s of stress and mental fatigue by ten and you might be getting somewhere near to what you will experience during training. Working days in the Corps are long and there is much to learn. You are doing the right thing by doing your homework, the more you know now the easier things will be in the long run. The amount of classroom work shocked me and everyone struggles to keep up with the curve. Spend time now increasing your brain power, learning memory techniques and start keeping reference files now. There is so much more to this than I have touched on here so please check out my soon to be released book 'Elite minds for Elite Forces' also by the Renegade Bootneck.

6 – Inclement weather

Joining the Royal Marines brought a whole new meaning to words 'bad weather'. Growing up on the Pennine hills, I was no stranger to all kinds of bizarre and extreme weather but often we would, stand, keep warm and say things like; 'Hey up, this weather is bizarre!' and ' By eck, that sideways hail stone is a bit extreme innit?'. As a Royal Marine, I soon learned that operating well during these conditions was a whole different ball game.

As civvies we are rarely exposed to bad weather for sustained periods. We always seem to know that we can nip indoors after a while and even when I was playing rugby on cold icy pitches, I could always look forward to a hot shower and clean, warm clothes. We were lucky enough to have temperatures as low as -13 when we were stood still for days in a trench and 40+ when we were doing the 30 miler. Training rarely stops for bad weather and it is ESSENTIAL you learn the skills to deal with all types of weather.

7 – Hot weather

Hot weather can also have horrendous effects on the body. Hyperthermia, heat exhaustion and severe dehydration are regular occurrences and have caused many deaths. Learn to recognise the effects of dehydration and ensure you remain hydrated at all times.

8 – Hunger

There are many restrictions in place nowadays to prevent you from suffering from hunger and thirst, but it is inevitable that you will at different points within training feel the extreme effects of both. Royal Marines training is renowned for being extremely calorie demanding and at CTC a fourth meal known as 'nine o'clockers', is laid on and apparently paid for by the queen to ensure recruits get all the calories they require. Not only do I recommend that you take steps to recognise the signs and symptoms of both hunger and thirst, but I recommend you get used to keeping your body fed and watered consistently. More specific nutritional advice can be found in the 'Nutrition for Nods' hand book, also by the Renegade Bootneck.

9 – Thirst

Get used to drinking lots of water now! I still get ribbed for carrying a water bottle everywhere I go and do so purely because I understand the health benefits of remaining hydrated and have experienced, first hand, just how severely performance is affected by dehydration. Many people have and will continue to fail the commando tests and the many fitness tests running up to the tests because they have failed to fuel or hydrate their bodies.

10 – Homesickness, boredom and worry.

Even the toughest hombre will suffer from homesickness, boredom and worry. Dislocation from your loved ones is tough enough without the stresses of basic training. I suggest spending some time away from your family as well as learning to be self-sufficient. Knowing you can cope will be a real comfort for you and your parents.

"I have two sons, one 19 and the 22, both either doing or done degrees. Both are thoroughly disillusioned with the job market and their prospects, and both seriously contemplating following their old man into the Corp. My advice to them and anyone else is get as fit as you can prior to joining and learn how to do the admin; wash 'iron, spit and polish etc etc etc. Life's hard enough without being up all night trying to get a tram line out your Lovet trousers or spit and polishing Parade boots! Oh yes! Don't piss off the PTI"

A, Former Bootneck PTI

Section 2.2 – Mental preparation.

The Commando mind-set or 'state of mind', to quote a recent recruitment strap line, needs to be the first thing you develop and I will help you. The correct state of mind will be key to your success. If you have it, then you are far more likely to succeed and pass the selection process.

As an example I will recall an event that I remember quite vividly from my time in training. I had been on exercise with the rest of my troop for a few days on a training area called Perridge Estate. It was the middle of winter and the UK was experiencing some record low temperatures. The exercise was predominantly to teach and practice patrolling skills. I was sat shivering in one of the many field practice periods that nods have during training and I just could not get warm.

The temperature had dropped to -13 and my feet were painfully sore with the cold. Though I struggled with many aspects of training I held my own on exercise and during field craft lessons and my section corporal soon realised I wasn't quite myself. He recognised the symptoms of hypothermia and ordered me to run up and down a track and to do star jumps to help get the blood flowing again and raise my body temperature. It took every ounce of effort and self-motivation not to throw the towel in there and then. I subsequently learnt that I had suffered Frost Nip on my feet where the top layers of skin had started to freeze.

The condition is common in polar explorers and causes incredible pain in the affected area. I was given the choice of either cracking on and fighting through or going back to the sick bay at Lympstone. Going back would most certainly mean I would be back trooped so thankfully I carried on.

Had I been lacking the self-motivation and tough commando spirit, I would have best case, back trooped to another troop behind ours in training or worse case, died of hypothermia. That all sounds dramatic, but seriously… how would you have reacted? And that was just one of many times during training when I had to search my soul for the energy and desire to carry on.

There are core qualities that every Royal Marine must have in abundance and each one makes up what is known as the Royal Marine ethos or Commando Spirit.

Royal Marines Ethos
Courage
Unity
Determination

Adaptability
Unselfishness
Humility
Cheerfulness in the face of adversity
Professional Standards
Fortitude
Commando Humour

Self-motivation

Wanting to do something and motivating yourself to actually do it are two different things. So, what's the difference between those who fail Royal Marines training and those who proudly accept their Green Berets after 32 week? Often, it's their self-motivation.

Self-motivation is the force that keeps pushing us to go on – it's our internal drive to achieve, produce, develop, and keep moving forward. When you think you're ready to quit something, or you just don't know how to start, your self-motivation is what pushes you to go on.

You are gonna need a lot of self-motivation! I would start be taking time to really think about WHY you want to join the Marines?

People join for a whole host of different reasons ranging from the fact they want to be the best, to following in their father's footsteps… but if you are simply saying 'well I don't really know what else to do!'

Recruits that do not have deep rooted personal reasons for pursuing a Green Beret to motivate themselves rarely succeed. My cousin applied to join the Marines, but had no real reason for joining other than he thought it would be cool to earn a Green Beret. That desire just was not enough to drive him through the PRMC let alone basic training.

Put some time aside right now to ask yourself why you want to join and list the reasons on a blank piece of paper. You may find the reasons come easily which is great and already oozes self-motivation, but if not, don't worry. It doesn't mean you are screwed. Just think about it all little harder and eventually they will come.

Once you have listed all the deep rooted reasons for joining the Marines you need to use those reasons to form very powerful mental images of how you will look, feel and be once you achieve your goals.

If you simply crave the Green Beret and see training as a personal challenge then imagine being handed your beret and putting it on for the first time. As you place the coveted cloth on your head, imagine the tears of pride in you mothers eyes and the how tall your dad stands as he watches you overcome the single biggest challenge of your life.

Whatever the reasons are, use them to form motivational images and think about them every time you train, every time someone tells you that you are mental for even trying or that you won't make it and eventually every time the training team test you during training.

With strong self-motivation, you'll start to develop the confidence that Royal Marines ooze. This confidence is often mistaken for arrogance, but comes from the knowledge that you have the motivation to crack on… even during the toughest times imaginable. That's why self-motivation is such a fundamental tool that you need to achieve your dreams and succeed.

Complete and uncompromising commitment

In 1519, Hernan Cortés landed with a fleet of 12 ships near present day Veracruz, Mexico. The flotilla held 500 Spaniards, 300 natives, a dozen horses and a few cannons. Cortés' aim was to conquer the Aztec Empire and take possession of its great wealth.

The legend is that before launching the attack Cortés burned his ships to prevent his men from retreating. Through the ages this brazen act has come to represent fully committing to a course of action. Going all in… or… burning all bridges.

Joining Her Majesty's finest is going to take complete and uncompromising commitment. You cannot go at this half-cocked. Here's how to get started in your complete commitment to getting your green beret.

1 – Tell everyone…

Tell all your friends, family and acquaintances that you are joining the Royal Marines. Some may take the piss, others will tell you that denim jackets will be fashionable before you get a green lid and that is exactly what you want. Tell them you will do it and prove them wrong. Then when things get tough and you think about quitting your mind will skip back to all those that joked… the ones you simply couldn't face if you gave in!

2 – Ditch the dead-end job.

You are destined for one of the greatest job in the world. You don't need that Saturday job cooking burgers in a fast food place. Ditch it and make it known that you WILL NOT be back.

3 – Concentrate the majority of your efforts on the task ahead.

Right now you have many interests and high on your list of priorities is chasing women, getting laid and socialising with your mates. That, coupled with hanging with your mates, gaming, surfing the web and Face 'Spacing' you probably do not have a lot of time to prepare yourself fully for joining the Royal Marines. The third step is to cut away some of the crap in your life. God knows, even in my day, when only the rich and gifted had mobiles and games consoles, there were enough distractions to fill the whole day full of shite. The trouble is no amount of Call of Duty will help you get up the 30 ft ropes or get you through the 30 miler.

Don't *spend* time… *invest* it!

Take a long hard look at where you **spend** your time. I say spend, because just like money, you WILL NOT get the time you spend tossing it off with your buddies or talking to Yanks while playing Modern Warfare all night. Look to **invest** you time learning the skills and theory that will help get you through training. Downloading the Bootneck Blueprint is a great first step, but simply reading this will NOT maximise your chances. You need to take action… otherwise you are likely to be the one heading home because you cannot keep up.

Teens are spending an increasing amount of time on digital media and it's raising rapidly each year. Teens and young adults simply do not spend the same amount of time outdoors, playing sports, learning new practical skills or experiencing hardships that I did… and I was still out of my depth during training!

Reality check

I am not saying completely cut every distraction from your life and live like a Buddhist monk until you hit Lympstone, but seriously think about where you SPEND your time and start to INVEST a little of it in your goals. If you could reduce your distractions even a little and INVEST 2 hours a day in your preparation for becoming a Commando, you will be head and shoulders over the other lads in your troop.

"You don't need to be the fittest nod, or the most switched on nod to be successful. What you do need is to be a people person and learn to engage your brain before your mouth, doing what you are told when you are told to do it (not cracking your own routine) and digging out for your fellow nods. If you do this, you should get through because the other nods will dig out .for you and the training team will cut you some slack. Yes you have to pass the criteria tests yourself, but adhering to the above will make your life so much easier. Trust me, I learned the hard way."

M, Former Bootneck PTI

Section 2.3 – Education.

I have already alluded to the fact that education is going to be a huge part of your development into a Commando in the Royal Marines. Listed below are the things I wish I had learnt before I hit Lympstone in the hope that the learning curve is not quite as steep for you as it was for me.

Warning – This is NOT going to be a full list of military skills and theory.

If I was to put everything you will learn throughout the 32 weeks in this book you would be faced with an overwhelming task of reading, learning processing and remembering that information.
Although you can prepare yourself in many ways, I suggest you leave the theory lessons to 'just in time' learning. Remember training is tough, but progressive. You learn the things you need to learn... just in time' to put it into practice.

Corps history

First up... the Royal Marines has a very long and prestigious history that you cannot possibly remember verbatim, but you can learn the basics. If I had invested time in learning just a few key dates as well as other bits of information, I could have avoided spending lots of time doing extra drill and extra parades!

"Sgt K..... always told us to "Remain flexible, and at all times retain your sense of humor". At the time I just thought he was a sadistic little twat who enjoyed making us poor little nods suffer. However since this little mantra has been quoted by me a million times ever since, on many occasions (the Mrs finishes it now, every time I start to say it...), I have come to realise what a wise man he really was. It was certainly a bit of advice that helped me get through it!"

D, Former Bootneck

"Before stepping off the train you need to develop a sense of humor that is deep, dark and self-mocking. Couple this to a mental resilience and bloody minded determination a never give up attitude and the ability to grin when there is really nothing to grin about and you will be off to a good start.

Clearly not everybody can develop the above and there is a huge genetic advantage if you are predisposed to that type of lunacy before signing on the dotted line. Another quote in here is spot on, identifying self-sacrifice and good old fashioned solid team work, an element lacking in some areas of civilian life."

A, Former Bootneck

Corps memorable dates

Another dead cert to crop up in many military knowledge tests and I guarantee your Drill Leader will love grilling you about the following during drill lessons.

The Birth of the Corps - 28 October 1664

It was Charles 2nd who ordered the first marine regiment, titled "the Duke of York and Albany's Maritime regiment of Foot". This Duke was the head of the Admiralty at the time. They wore yellow jackets due to the allegiance to said Duke (it was his favourite colour), and is why there is a yellow stripe on the corps colours today. There were 1200 men in this new regiment, raised to fight the Dutch at sea in the Second Dutch war.

The Capture of the Rock of Gibraltar - 24 July 1704

This attack took place in conjunction with the Dutch Marines (and 3 Commando Brigade retains a strong links to the Netherlands Marine Corps to this day). A total force 2300 marines (1900 British) took the Rock and defended it during the 9 month siege that followed. This is the only battle honour display on the colours and crest.

The Battle of Belle Isle - 7 June 1761

The Marines played a major role in the capture of this island, from the first amphibious landing, and through all subsequent fighting. The laurel wreath borne on the colours, crest and cap badge of the Marines is believed to have been adopted in honour of the distinguished service of the Corps during this operation.

The Battle of Trafalgar - 21 October 1805

Around 3000 Royal Marines were present at Nelson's famous victory over the French and Spanish. Fighting on the upper decks, they suffered heavy casualties on the leading ships but formed the core of the boarding parties that succeeded in capturing so many enemy ships.

The Raid on Zeebrugge - 23 April 1918

This operation was to deny the Germans the use of the canal at Zeebrugge, a port in Belgium, that was conducted jointly between the navy and the Marines. The objective was successfully achieved, with troops landing on the Mole under heavy fire and positions held to allow others time to block the canal. Two Victoria Crosses were awarded, by ballot, to Marines following this operation.

The Normandy landings - 6 June 1944

Marines played a huge role in this operation, manning most landing craft, providing specialist groups (e.g. mine clearance), manning guns on support ships and the commandos of course leading the assault itself. In total 16,000 marines took part in Operation Overload.

Recapture of the Falklands - 14 June 1982

Royal Marines based in the Falklands were the first to come across Argentine invaders, and succeeded in killing around 30enemy (including the destruction of an AMTRAK vehicle) before being overrun, at no loss to themselves. Subsequently the Marines dispatched from Britain played a leading role in the campaign, manning all landings. Marines then yomped across a large part of East Falklands to take part in the battle for the main town, Port Stanley. Successes in the mountains around Stanley for the Marines led to the Argentine surrender. Approximately 50% of the corps as it existed in 1982 took part on this campaign.

The Royal Marines have been subsequently involved in Operations in Northern Ireland (since well before 1969), the jungles of Indo-China (e.g. Malaya) fighting communist insurgents in the 1960s, Northern Iraq (Operation Haven following Desert storm) in 1991, The Balkans (e.g. Kosovo from 1999) and of course have been heavily involved in the Afghanistan conflict since 2001, and also the Iraq war 2003-2009.

Basic Military knowledge

Field craft

Royal Marines can boast that they can not only live in ANY environment but can fight in any environment. The foundation of this ability is established through field exercises and practice sessions on Woodbury Common near Lympstone to establish basic field craft.

Listed below are a few of the key field craft elements that you could learn and practice prior to starting RT. REMEMBER… don't try to learn everything, you will become overwhelmed. Field craft will cover everything from living and taking care of yourself in the field to locating and engaging the enemy and pretty much everything in between.

You will learn how to use your eyes to see better in the dark, how to improve your observation and hearing and how to move without being compromised. Look out for field craft related posts at royalmarinestraining.com

Map reading

A fundamental and often neglected skill within the forces is map reading. The heavy reliance in modern technology has had a dramatic effect on how modern soldiers do business. For some, learning to map read is not an attractive prospect, for those wishing to join the Marines… it is essential.

What follows below is a number of essential elements you would do well to learn now. They WILL come up in military knowledge tests and the like and you can dramatically reduce the learning curve by learning these hot tips now. Watch out for map reading related posts at royalmarinestraining.com or look for the **Nod Navigation Handbook** also by the Renegade Bootneck, to help increase your practical knowledge about map reading.

Ensure you study and become proficient in the following:

- The definition of a map
- The care of a map
- Aids to navigation
- Components of a map
- Types of scale and where they can be found on a map
- Conventional signs
- The grid system
- How to take and plot a bearing
- How to work out the GMA
- How to find your location using a re-section

Weapons

To get started you don't need much more than the ability to recognise the basic troop weapons used by the Royal Marines, including:

- Sa80 A2
- 51mm mortar
- Long Range Rifle
- GPMG
- Minimi
- Under slung Grenade Launcher
- NLAW
- L109 Grenades

"Don't break your ribs 6 weeks before you start! Serious point was I would have started to prepare myself a lot earlier and not just on the phys front. Stop arse-ing around on the rugby pitch, start focusing on months of physical and mental trauma, start learning how to iron, polish, make a bed and learn all the other things that you never realised made up being a Bootneck probably by having a chat with one."

K, Former Bootneck Officer

Signals

Learn the phonetic alphabet listed below. You'll be amazed at how many lads start training and don't know it inside out. PS… don't worry about the Morse code… that stuff is older than your dads favourite pants and is just about as useful!!

A – Alpha
B – Bravo
C – Charlie
D – Delta
E – Echo
F – Foxtrot
G – Golf
H – Hotel
I – India
J – Juliet
K – Kilo
L – Lima
M – Mike
N – November
O – Oscar
P – Papa
Q – Quebec
R – Romeo
S – Sierra
T – Tango
U – Uniform
V – Victor
W – Whiskey
X – Xray
Y – Yankee
Z - Zulu

Ranks and roles

Learn the basic ranks from recruit to Warrant Officer 1 and at least 2nd lieutenant to Lieutenant Colonel.

Administration

Learning the basic administration principles of the military will dramatically reduce the learning curve for you during recruit training. Look out for video tutorials on RoyalMarinesTraining.com.

Specifically you need to learn:

- Hospital corners and bed making
- Boot polishing including 'bulling' aka 'spit and polish'
- Hand washing clothes
- Ironing
- How to fold clothes to A4 size

Personal administration

Personal administration basically equates to being able to look after yourself to prevent injury, illness and maintain personal hygiene.

Specifically you need to learn how to:

- Wash, shower and shave,
- Prevent and treat blisters
- Prevent and treat friction burns aka 'webbing burns'

Part Three

Preparing the Body

Part Three

Section 3.1: Preparing the body

During my time in the Corps and on recruit training teams I was struck by just how much emphasis was placed on physical ability. Personally I believe a Marine should be judged on your professionalism in the field and your soldiering ability. A high standard of physical fitness should be a bolt on of that. There is no denying however that a high level of fitness is going to be essential in your chances of success.

I would suggest that 90 – 95% of people that want to join the Marines do so because they want to challenge themselves and win a green beret. To win the Green Beret you have to complete the Commando tests and too many young recruits focus purely on the physical. Do so at your peril.

Getting started

You MUST prepare your body completely for basic training, but you need to be more than fitter, faster and stronger. There are many facets of fitness and you will need to nurture every one of them to succeed in training.

We have the 12 week training programme available at royalmarinestraining.com, which is a blend of the latest sports science coupled with the deepest RM basic training PT secrets, produced by our Renegade PTI. This program alone will increase your chance of success tenfold.

But here are the secrets that PTI's do NOT want you to know.

Basic training has changed now. Society no longer allows the systematic bullying and 'thrashing' of recruits to break them. PT is structured to be progressive so that, as long as you begin with a certain level of fitness, remain uninjured and recover well, you will be more than ready to complete the Commando tests when they come around.

I have seen recruits pass out that freely admit that they did very little physical training before joining up and do well but do you want to take that chance? As with everything, you can make things hard or you can make things easy. I would advocate the easy route! Investing in your physical preparation in a structured, specific and progressive program, such as the 12 training plan available to you at plan will truly maximise your chances of passing out.

Initial tests and feedback from the 12 week training programme suggest that the program is so effective it can take an average, moderately active lad, and develop their fitness to a level that would easily cope with the rigors of basic training – In 6 weeks! In 12 weeks the program will have you maxing out on ALL the gym tests.

Physiology of a Bootneck

Your body has three main energy systems and fitness within the corps will require each one to be highly tuned and effective. The Creatine phosphate system will provide the explosive strength to jump, sprint and haul your way through the Tarzan assault course. The anaerobic system will allow fuel your lengthy press up or fireman's carry sessions and the aerobic system will trickle feed your muscles with the energy required for perpetual running. You will need to be able to tap into these energy systems throughout your basic training so you will need to train each of these systems equally. Do not fall foul to the same mistake that many do and train within your comfort zone, within one specific energy system and one mode of training. Structured variety is the key to covering all bases.

Through my research for this book I found that many lads joining up nowadays are split training into either cardio and what they perceive as (it usually isn't) strength work. You need to kind of throw it all together. Your training cannot be based heavily around endurance work of long runs because you need the upper body strength to haul your arse up the ropes, carry your oppo or do the 100 press ups you got cos you fucked up. Not only do you need the ability to haul yourself up a 30 foot wall with all your kit, but you have to have the endurance to get through everything else to get to the wall.

You will also need many of the other facets such as speed, agility, balance, coordination and proprioception and coupled with all that you need to build some ruggedness within your body. You need to condition yourself to handle the rigors that your whole body will be put through. I am not just talking about the obvious shock through your feet and knees through miles of running in boots along tar mac country roads, but the battering your knees will take in the tunnels of the endurance course and the constant rubbing of ill-fitting kit. You will need to harden your bones, muscles, tendons and areas that are susceptible to blisters. You must also have the stability and flexibility to withstand muscle strains when slipping in wet and muddy conditions or twisting an ankle on uneven ground.

OK – Some absolute no-no's

You are fucking wasting your time doing body building routines. If you are training now to increase mass you have fucked up massively. Regardless of how good you want to look on the beach, in the night club with your low cut top and jeans hanging off your arse, body building routines are extremely detrimental to your quest to gain your green beret. Body building routines in the gym are designed to build mass and people forget that they must then carry that weight! I remember an ex doorman I was in training with who looked like a 'universal soldier' until he hit leafy lane! Then he turned into a slobbering, dehydrated mess.

My advice to you with regard to body building routines is STOP NOW. Anything that smells of body building such as 3 sets of ten, drop sets, pyramid sets, bicep curls, triceps extensions or any exercise that works muscle in isolation are a waste of time for you. Yes there is a place for isolation exercises if you are injured or have a deficit in a larger exercise and wish to break a sticking point. I.e. if your pull ups are shit and you strain like a shitting dog when you try getting your chin over the bar, then there is a case to work on the smaller muscles to assist. So building grip strength or specific bicep strengthening exercises may help. Similarly, if your press ups are dog shit, tri-cep strengthening movements may be the answer.

If you are conducting isolation exercises to get fit for the Corps then you are wasting your time. In a similar fashion, if you are running like a 14 year old Kenyan school boy and doing 14 mile a day to and from school, then you are way of course. Running to that extent will cause a catabolic (muscle wasting) effect on your muscles and you won't have the strength required for pull ups and the like. Also, if you are running to that extent you run the risk of picking up RSI injuries such as stress fractures in the shins or muscle tears and ligament damage.

You also need to make your body move in an efficient manner so that you are not running or doing press ups and the like with dog shit technique.

Believe it or not there is a scientific approach to PT in basic training. Even before my time there was an attitude of 'just thrash the muthas until they break and get rid of the crap'. The idea back then was thrash the hell out of them to get the numbers down and then mould what's left in the second fifteen weeks of training. For recruits it was a case of hanging in there for as long as possible and hope you have the luck needed not to get injured. Training is now structured so every recruit is ready for the tests when they arrived. In my time it was a case of running recruits down so they are physically knackered for the Commando tests.

It is basically a case of you getting to Lympstone and getting through the PRMC in a fit enough state to begin the structured process of getting you Commando fit. In all honesty the basic foundation is not elite in any way. It is easy to ascertain and available to anyone that wants to put their heart into it and work hard. Many people arrive at Lymstone with mediocre fitness levels and scrape through by the skin of their teeth. Hey! They get through and fair play to them, but why just scrape through and leave a lot to chance? Many go to the PRMC and say it was the hardest thing they have ever done, well it's gonna be. This is the selection process for one of the world's toughest forces. What do you expect? Also, my greatest physical tests came after basic training in things that bizarrely I volunteered for.

To summarise, your training must be supported by good nutrition and must be efficient and specific to what you are trying to achieve.

"Fear and self-doubt is harboured by all. You will not be alone as you step off the train, sweaty palmed and legs trembling, but you are about to undergo a process. A process of reducing self-doubt and gaining self-confidence. Later civvies, members of the Navy and RAF will mistake this confidence for an over inflated ego, not the supreme confidence you now command having conquered many challenges. I am not talking over inflated egos like the US Marine corps 'best of the best of the best shit… 'One day you will have the calm confidence in your abilities, the good news is you can start to nurture that now in anticipation for training."

The Renegade Bootneck

Further resources

http://prmcprep.com **– Specialist course to prepare you for the PRMC**
http://royalmarinestraining.com **– The very best Royal Marines recruitment advice and home of the Royal Marines Blueprint Podcast**
http://bootneckblueprint.com **– Download the complete eBook and the 2 week panic PT programme**
http://bootneckblueprint.com/rnrt/ **- Royal Navy Recruitment test sample questions**

Printed in Great Britain
by Amazon